Local Search Marketing for Business:
A How- To

Published by VM Press, Phoenix, Arizona.

No part of this publication may be reproduced…

ISBN: 1-4565-4819-0
ISBN-13: 9781456548193

Local Search Marketing for Business: A How- To

Sarah Moraes

VERTICAL MEASURES

Edited by: Michael Shwartz
Cover design or artwork by: David Gould
Editorial coordination by: Elise Redlin-Cook

2011

Dedication

I dedicate this book first and foremost to my dog, Koko. A dog is loyal and without the ability to judge. He lay by my side for many hours during the creation of this book. I must also acknowledge my best friend, Daniel Yelick, who never fails to push me further and challenge me to do better. And finally, thank you to my unconditionally loving and supportive family, the Moraes'.

TABLE OF CONTENTS

Prologue

"Local is huge." You've probably heard this a few times by now, hence why you decided to pick up this handy guide. When most prospects or clients come to us asking for local search marketing, the number one issue that we run into is that they are treating it as a separate entity and are terrified to make any changes to their website that might somehow destroy their rankings. But, in fact, search engines are actually penalizing websites that are not making those very changes. Further, a business can easily integrate a local search strategy into its current online marketing plan and reap great benefits.

When I was asked to write this How to Guide to Local Search Marketing, I thought to myself, OK but what if by the time the book is published, everything has changed? That is the nature of Internet marketing. There are no concrete answers and what answers you do find, are not really answers but well-supported theories. Local search is especially unpredictable. But, when I started to put this guide together, I realized that there are principles that have mostly stayed the same and can easily be adapted to meet the ever changing landscape.

This guide provides a holistic view of local search marketing, integrating multiple disciplines including; on-site optimization, link building, social media and other Internet marketing tactics. No longer can local search be treated as a separate strategy. It is my hope that Local Search: a How to Guide provides businesses with a roadmap to implement a local search campaign that drives traffic not only to their website, but directly to their place of business. As the guide was developed with a variety of skill sets in mind, it is written in such a way that businesses will be able to easily apply the information given to their current search engine optimization and marketing plans.

Chapter 1
Local Search Marketing for Business

To fully grasp the concept of local search marketing, simply think of how you search for products and services online. When you are looking to purchase a pair of shoes, a car or need a haircut, what do you type into the search box? It is likely something like this: Scottsdale running shoe store, San Francisco Audi dealer, or Boston hair salons. You might even get more specific and type in a postal code or neighborhood. This is in fact, how most people are conducting their online searches today. The figures vary, but are all relatively saying the same thing. Google states that over 20% of searches conducted on the search engine have local intent. In addition, across all search engines, it has been estimated that over 80% of searches are geospecific, meaning that the search query includes a geographic modifier like the examples above.

Local is huge...period. Google's US ad revenue is roughly $15 billion and the size of the US Yellow Pages market is approximately $14 billion. While most of that money is still allocated to print advertising, the shift to online local marketing is accelerating with Google's emphasis on localized results.

In the past, consumers relied upon traditional means such as that big brick called the Yellow Pages or the local newspapers to find local products and services. With the increased use of the Internet across all demographics, consumers are increasingly using search engines to find these local businesses online. In recent years, the number of local searches online has grown rapidly while off-line information searches, such as print Yellow Page lookups, have declined. With this shift in consumer behavior, local product and service providers are shifting their advertising dollars and efforts from traditional off-line media to local search engines.

The Yellow Pages is updated every few months, but today, the Yellow Pages can be found on the Internet, which is updated every second! Local search provides instant satisfaction to a customer. For example, a customer hoping to find a service locally would much rather have a map show up with directions to their destination rather than have to search for an address that is buried deep within a website.

And with much of the world switching to iPhones and Androids, the local search industry is going to continue to grow. According to Google's Jonathan Rosenberg, mobile ads are already a billion dollar market for Google. Consumers are demanding on the spot information and local search provides that to them. It tells them exactly where the closest Starbucks is, the closest computer repair shop, the closest Toyota dealer, plumber, cleaning service, and so on.

Businesses must adapt to modern consumer behavior, as it will only continue to move online. There are of course, socioeconomic groups that do not engage heavily in online activity or simply cannot afford to. But, technology is increasingly becoming more affordable and there are many programs that are making cell phones and computers more accessible.

Certain industries get more geospecific searches than others do. A recent Nielsen study with Comscore and TMP Directional Marketing in 2008 revealed how people are searching based on industry category.

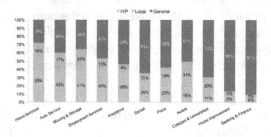

Not only should business operators be paying attention to this accelerated shift, but SEOs too. Gone are the days that local and organic SEO were seen as two different animals. Today, it is one enormous beast.

This how to guide to local search marketing for businesses will provide the following:

- Insight to the local search marketing industry as it stands today
- How to determine which geospecific keywords to target
- Best practices for a properly optimized website
- Steps to claiming and optimizing search engine listings
- Tips to build up your online presence with citations, reviews and link building
- Solutions for businesses that serve customers at their homes or in the field

The Local Search Marketing Industry

The History of Google Local Search

Google has a very cool time line of corporate milestones, that it updates every so often with the changes and new products it rolls out.

Here are the instances that had to do with Google Local and Google Maps.

March 2004: Google introduced Google Local, offering relevant neighborhood business listings, maps and directions.

February 2005: Google Maps was released and featured satellite views and directions. Shortly after that, Google Local was available for mobile devices and included SMS driving directions.

June 2005: Google Earth, a satellite imagery-based mapping service combining 3D buildings and terrain with mapping capabilities and Google search, is unveiled.

February 2007: Traffic information introduced for Google Maps for more than 30 cities around the US.

May 2007: Street View debuts in Google Maps in five U.S. cities: New York, San Francisco, Las Vegas, Miami and Denver.

June 2007: Google Maps gets prime placement on the original Apple iPhone.

June 2008: A new version of Maps for Mobile debuts, putting Google Transit directions on phones in more than 50 cities worldwide.

June 2009: Google adds a new dashboard to Google Places, which gives business owners information, such as what people searched for to see their listing or how many times their listing appeared in search results, about how customers find their businesses in Google Maps.

September 2009: Google introduces Place Pages to Google Maps: one page that organizes all the relevant information about a business, point of interest, transit station, neighborhood, landmark or city—in any part of the world—in one place. Place Pages include rich details, like photos, videos, a Street View preview, nearby transit, reviews and related websites.

October 2009: Google Maps Navigation, a turn-by-turn GPS navigation system, includes 3D views and voice guidance—and because it's connected to the Google cloud, it always includes the newest map data, lets you search by voice or along a route, and provides live traffic data.

April 2010: Google Places (formerly the Local Business Center) gets a new name along with some new features, like showing service areas and, in some cities, the ability to use an easy advertising program called Tags.

Not yet officially listed on the timeline, in November 2010 Google's local results were mixed in with the organic results bringing local search to the forefront in the Internet marketing world.

Local search has evolved dramatically over the past few years as the demand for local businesses in search results has also increased dramatically. While things have changed, the message to local businesses is still the same. Local businesses must incorporate a well thought out local search marketing campaign into their overall marketing plan in order to be successful both online and offline.

Chapter 2
Consumer Behavior

A popular image often shown in presentations given by SEOs and Internet marketers is a heat map showing where people click on the page of search results. Most of the clicks are at the top left of the page on listings one or two of the search results. And, if a heat map was shown of page two or three, there are virtually no clicks or traffic. So what does this have to do with local search marketing?

As shown in the previous timeline, in November 2010, Google combined the local and organic search results. This means that all consumer behavior associated with organic search results should essentially apply to that of the new combined results. The local results used to most commonly be called the 7-pack. When a searcher conducted a geospecific search, Google would display seven local results as determined by a separate algorithm than the organic results, along with a map to the right of those seven businesses.

In an eye tracking study conducted by Sentient Services for the local 7-pack, it showed similar results as the heat map for organic results. So one can assume that the results for the organic local or local organic, whatever you prefer to call these combined results, will be the same.

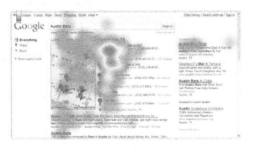

This research and this report are © 2010, ionadas local LLC and Sentient Services, LP. They are being published under a Creative Commons Attribution 3.0 license, allowing businesses, organizations and individuals to download, use and reproduce the data in their own promotional and research efforts providing proper attribution is made.

Consumers are online and they are not just passively searching for businesses but actively engaging and talking about local businesses. With sites like Yelp, Foursquare, Gowalla, and Merchant Circle, consumers are "checking-in" and "Yelping" about businesses, providing ratings and reviews. Yelp was founded in 2004 to help people find local businesses, but didn't really take off until recent years. As of August 2010, more than 38 million people visited Yelp in just the past 30 days. In addition, more than 12 million local reviews have been written by Yelp users. Yelp updates these stats every so often on its website. Of course the numbers continue to grow.

Here are a few other milestones and statistics that should drive home just how important it is to engage in local search marketing:

- Google announced that there are over four million claimed Places Pages worldwide, two million of which are in the U.S.
- Facebook Places arrived in August 2010
- Foursquare came onto the scene in 2009.
- Foursquare announced on Dec. 1, 2010, that it had over 5 million users.
- According to a study by Comscore based on 2008/2009 data, local search grew 46% over that year while general search grew 31%. 80% of consumers expect businesses in their search result to be within 15 miles of their location. 70% of all searches have local intent.

A more recent study conducted by BIA/Kelsey's Group stated that:

- "Nearly all consumers (97 percent) now use online media when researching products or services in their local area...Among consumers surveyed, 90 percent use search engines, 48 percent use Internet Yellow Pages, 24 percent use vertical sites, and 42 percent use comparison shopping sites."

As you can see, between the time that the Comscore study was conducted and the Kelsey's Group study was conducted...the numbers have skyrocketed. Local search can no longer be swept under the rug. Local search is what's happening.

What these numbers and events are telling us is that consumers want local businesses. Consumers are searching for the local bike shop, the local Chinese restaurant and the local hair stylist. Be where your customers are, online.

Chapter 3
It All Starts With Onsite Optimization

The organo-local search results are a combination of the results as determined by the organic algorithm and those determined by the local algorithm. This means that all of the factors that affect the organic search results essentially affect the local search results. There are other very important variables that affect local search rankings, which I will throughout this how-to guide.

Before a business takes on a local search marketing campaign and before an SEO or Internet marketing company takes on a client for local search marketing, the first and most important factor is on-site optimization.

If a website is poorly optimized and is engaging in black-hat practices, it should and will very likely be penalized, pushing it back not only in the natural search results but now in the organo-local results.

The first three most important items that a local business must have is NAP, a commonly used industry acronym for Name + Address + Phone Number.

Business Name: A business must have an appropriate business name for the services and products it provides. An example of a business name that might affect its rankings is "Johnny's." Well, "Johnny's" what? If Johnny sells pizza or is a breakfast restaurant, something in the name of the business should convey that. Making just a slight change of the business' name can help significantly.

Address: Next, a local address is essential today to be listed in the Google organo-local search results. Whereas in the past, businesses may have created fake addresses, PO boxes, etc., these less than ethical practices will be penalized. This is one of the primary reasons that Google made the change that it did in how the local results were determined and displayed. A real, local address where the business can meet with customers and receive mail is critical. And what does this mean for businesses that service customers in the local areas at their home? The business should still have one local address where a business owner could meet with a customer if needed and also the business owner can receive mail. This should not be a PO Box.

8

Phone Number: And finally, the third equally important item that a local business must have is a local phone number. A business should avoid at all costs having only an 800 number.

With regards to tracking numbers, they don't mix well with local SEO. Having a tracked phone number can cause the search engines to become confused and possibly consider your one business, two businesses. For example, if you give your local phone number to Google, but you give your tracking phone number to a data aggregator and that tracking number is then picked up by Google, the search engine will very likely create two thumbprints. Data aggregators, covered in more depth later, are considered authoritative sources for the search engines.

These three items, Business Name, Address and Phone Number, should be displayed on every page of a website and should be formatted so that the web crawlers can find them. These items should not be placed as images.

Keyword Research

Localized content has become very important with local organic results. In order to create a localized content strategy, start with keyword research to determine which geospecific keywords a business' website should be optimized for.

There are many free tools to determine which keywords you should focus on for your business. The different tools at times will show different results. Here is a list of some great free tools that can be used together to determine the best keywords for your business.

- Google Insights
- Google AdWords
- SEOMoz.org
- Wordtracker Free Keyword Tool

Keyword research can very much be considered an art. James Constable, Vertical Measures Link Strategy Specialist, covers the topic in depth in his Keyword Research How to Guide for Businesses. Check out the guide before diving into this. The concepts still apply to local, but here are some specific things to keep in mind when choosing your geospecific keywords:

- Search Volume and Competition: A keyword that gets more searches isn't necessarily the best one. Choose keyword phrases that have middle-moderate search volume. Choosing keywords with extremely high search volume can make it impossible to rank due to the competition.

- Include Long Tail Keyword Phrases: People are searching for keyword phrases that are four and five words long and thus very specific, especially when a geographic modifier is included. You can cover more ground by including a short tail keyword phrase within a long tail phrase, maximizing your chance of getting picked up for various searches.
- Utilize your Google Places Dashboard to see what keywords people were searching for when they found your Places page.

Creating Localized Content

Localized content has never been more important to search engine optimization success than it is today. It is important not only to have a content strategy, but a localized content strategy as well. The purpose of a localized content strategy is to identify what content segments are unique to each geographical area and highlight those on a state level, city level and even micro level by building dedicated pages for these audiences. Here are some ideas for localized content:

Ideally, a company will have a page on its website for each location or service area that it does business in. For example, if a national pizza restaurant has three restaurants in Arizona—say Chandler, Tempe, and Scottsdale—it will have an Arizona option and then three pages, one for each city. You might think that this seems a bit redundant or pointless. Why not just have all of the addresses listed on one page? Because the search engines like content-rich websites filled with valuable information for the consumer. You should list more than an address. You should list location-specific information such as specials, happy hour information, images of the restaurant, images of recent events and even include information about the city in which the restaurant is located.

Additionally, here are more examples of the types of pages that can help the search engines as well as your visitors understand your business location.

- Directions pages: provide the customer directions from various nearby cities.
- Local community pages: information about the surrounding area and community.
- Resources pages for tourists: places to visit and dine when visiting you.
- Resources for homebuyers: provide nearby schools and parks for those looking to purchase a home in the area.

There are countless resources that businesses owners can provide for the website visitors. But, of course keep the information relevant and related to your business.

The company should optimize each of these pages for a geospecific key-word. For example, the Chandler page would likely be optimized for "Chandler pizza restaurant."

Keyword searches are tending to become longer. Rather than two or three keyword phrases, searchers are typing in three to four keyword phrases (not much of a difference between 2-3 and 3-4). These are often called longtail keywords. Consumers are getting very specific about what they want. Searches including four to five keywords are becoming more common than two to three keyword searches. Before you optimize your site, conduct your keyword research! There are many free tools out there that are included in the resources section of this book.

Keyword Meta Tags

Include your location and keywords in the page copy as well as links to the page you've optimized for local search. It isn't ideal to use your homepage as the page optimized for local search unless you only do business in your local area. Your homepage is better utilized as a landing page for broader, non location-specific queries, so in most cases your Contact page or another similar page will be better suited for local searches since it already includes your location's address and infor-mation.

Image and Video Optimization

Including images on both your website as well as your local search listings is vital to ranking in the search results and provides for a better consumer experience when they visit your website. Images bring life to your business and will leave an impression on your visitor. If they see an image of your storefront and then drive by your storefront, they will likely remember it. Optimizing your images is equally important. You should include alt tags for each image. Alt tags are the text that is displayed behind the image or will display when the image is not available. The search engines use this text to identify what the image is.

Microformats

Rich Snippets

Incorporating rich snippets into your website structure is a great way to tell the search engines exactly what content is location-specific on your website. Google announced this feature on their Webmaster blog back in 2009 and with the prominence of the organo-local search results today, it's important to incorporate this code into your website.

Straight from that very blog post, "…Rich Snippets [is] a new presentation of snippets that applies Google's algorithms to highlight structured data embedded in web pages."

When Google first introduced Rich Snippets they only supported data about reviews and people. Recently Rich Snippet support has grown to include much more than that, such as specific geographic information about a business' location including the business name, phone number and address.

So how does this affect the way your business is displayed in the search results? When a user searches for a product or service, by marking up your address, phone number and other important location-based information you're improving your chances that this is the exact information Google will display. By annotating the pages of your site with the structured data using the standard microformat given by Google, users will see the information you've marked from a particular page. It is, however, important to note that there are no guarantees that everything you mark up will be displayed. Google, of course, will adhere to its algorithm and policies to determine the relevant snippets to include for each query.

To display Rich Snippets, Google looks for markup formats (microformats and RDFa) that can easily be added to your own web pages. In most cases, it is simply wrapping existing data on your web pages with some additional tags.

To see exactly what Google is able to extract and validate your code, Google offers a handy Rich Snippets Testing Tool. It will provide you with a preview of how your information may appear in the search results and feedback if setup incorrectly. http://www.google.com/webmasters/tools/richsnippets

Reviews

Including customer reviews and testimonials on your site provides valuable content to your visitors. So, the search engines will give you points for that. In addition, you can mark up your reviews to show the search engines which reviews to display from your website in the search results. Again, it's not guaranteed they will be displayed, but if a user is searching for reviews relevant to your business, why not take the time to better your chance of having the reviews you're proud of show up, versus perhaps some other negative reviews?

Chapter 4
Google Places and Other Search Engine Listings

Google Places

This is one of the variations of the search results that users are seeing today when local search results are displayed. The paid listings are at the top in blue. A map to the right is above locally targeted PPC results and moves down the screen as a user scrolls. Then, there are some Google Places listings and organic results in the main search results area. Very different from what we have seen previously.

Following keyword research and onsite optimization, the next important step is to set up or claim the business' Google Places listing.

There is an array of reasons as to why this is so important. First and foremost, competitors have been known to claim other business' listings and spam them or insert false information. A recent investigation found that locksmiths were adding their phone number to other business' online listings so that all of the phone calls would go to them, stealing business from the other locksmiths. To ensure this doesn't happen, businesses should follow the steps to claim and verify their Google Places listing as well as the other local search listings on the web.

Steps to Creating a Google Places Listing

Set up a Gmail Account: If already have a Gmail account, skip ahead to Step 2. If you don't, go to www.gmail.com. It is best to set up a dedicated email address for your local search as you will be receiving a lot of emails to verify your listings as well as regular emails that this listing sites send. I recommend your companyname@ gmail.com.

List Your Business: Once you are logged in, go to Google Places and arrive at this screen. If your business is not already listed, go to List Your Business. If you found your unclaimed listing, there will be a "Business Owner?" link at the top of the map listing that allows you to click it and go claim your listing.

You will then arrive at this page.

Ideally, you want to list a local phone number, not an 800 number because the search engines can use your phone number to recognize where your business is located and therefore more easily list your business in the local results for various queries in your area.

The Details: Google will check your phone number once more to see if they already have your information. Since they do not, you will come to this page where you can start to fill out your listing. The more information you can fill out this listing with, the better. Be sure to make sure it is accurate and matches the information on your website. In the description area, you will want to include up to 2-3 of your priority keywords. You will want to do this with all of your local search listings when possible and I will cover some other important listings later on. You only have 200 words for the description area, so it might be best to create a standard local search listing description as a template when creating your listings.

Categories: I am specifically talking about the Category aspect because it has been highlighted as one of the most important factors in the Google Local Search ranking algorithm. Take some time to think about the best categories for your business. This is actually required now whereas it did not used to be. That is how important your business categories are.

Website: Including your website is essential. While it is not required here, it should be! It is a link back to your website. Your customers need a way to get to your site. Make it easy for them.

Business Service Areas: When Google created the organo-local results, it became critical for a business to have an address. In the past, Google was not enforcing its own rules and guidelines, allowing for businesses such as plumbers and locksmiths to scam the system with false addresses and PO Boxes. Google Places is now strictly enforcing its rules and guidelines and has created a solution for businesses that serve customers at their homes or out in the field.

Under the Service Area and Location settings, it asks, "Does your business provide services, such as delivery or home repair, to location in a certain area?" There are two choices: "No, customers come to the business location" OR "Yes, this business services customers at their locations." If the answer is "No, customers come to the business location," then proceed to the next steps. If the answer is "Yes," this business services customers at their location.

A business does not have to allow the address used to create the listing to be visible, but there are varying opinions about what is ideal. If the business address is a home, then it is probably best to not make it visible. This will protect any family or friends living at that location from being bothered. If the business address is an office, it is ideal to go ahead and list it for maximum optimization and visibility. A visible address in a Google Places listing is an additional indicator to other search engines that the business has been verified and it matches what is listed on the business' website and in other listings.

To show customers where the business provides its services, Google Places has a field to list cities served. As cities are entered in this area, a red shadow will cover the area on the map.

Do not list cities that you don't service just to show up in the listings. This is providing a disservice not only to the person searching for the service but to the business owner when that person gets upset and writes a negative review on the listing calling the business out for doing this.

Distance from the Centroid: Something very important to keep in mind is that Google is going to show the results in the Map results that are closest to the centroid of the city being search. As determined by the local the search engines, the centroid is the very center of a neighborhood or metropolitan area. This is not something that a business owner can control and it is not worth engaging in black-hat practices in order to show up in cities in which you do not do business. The search engines have become very savvy to that behavior and are proactively penalizing those businesses.

Hours and Payment Option: Again, filling out your listing with valuable information is very important and will help your customers get to know your business.

Photos and Videos: The search engines love a variety of content on your website, so why wouldn't Google love photos and videos on your Places listing? Add relevant photos and videos to your business. Any photos or videos that would add to your website or YouTube channel are great content to add to your Google Places listing.

Additional Details: Any additional information that can be provided to customers will be both valuable for them and for your rankings. Include anything here that you feel is important for your potential customers to know when visiting your business.

When you're ready, click Submit. After you've submitted your listing, you will have two options to verify your listing. You can select to receive a phone call or a postcard with a PIN number that you will have to enter to verify your listing. The phone call is automated and has a series of prompts that an actual person must complete. So, be sure to notify anyone that picks up the phone at your business that this call is coming and is very important. When I'm setting up listings for clients, I usually opt for the postcard so it's easier for the business operator to get. Sometimes there are just too many employees and confusion associated with the phone call to make it clear. I simply send an email to the client and ask them to forward to their employees to call me with the PIN number. It has worked pretty well so far. However, this postcard can take 2-3 weeks to arrive, the only downfall.

Once you've confirmed your listing, you're ready to go!

If you have multiple locations, you can add up to 10 to Google Places. Be sure to add any information that is specific to these locations including the address, phone number, hours and products and services that might be unique to that location. This is also an opportunity to add some different keywords to each listing.

Google Places Dashboard

Once your listing is complete, the business owner will have a Google Places Dashboard.

From the dashboard, the business owner can update details of the listing, and add photos, videos, coupons and more. The Google Places Dashboard now contains important search data, making it an even more valuable tool. With this data, the business owner can determine which keywords users were searching for when they found the business, page visit data and even where customers are coming from geographically. This data can help to target the proper local areas and demographics for a business. This dashboard should not be used in place of a keyword research tool such as Wordtracker or Google AdWords, but in conjunction with those to ensure a business is constantly adapting to what searchers are doing.

Google Tags

Tags can now be applied to listings to make them more noticeable on the Google Places page and Google Maps. This can be a valuable tool in taking customers from Google Maps to the Place Page, so make sure the tags are carefully chosen and up to date.

A business can tag something such as a phone number or a particular service to make it stand out. It entices the customer to commit an action on your listing, to click on the phone number or the website link. Tags are certainly worth trying at just $25 per month. Whether or not they are effective long term is yet to be determined as they've only been around a short time. In addition, it's something that might work for some business or industries and not for others.

Google Boost

Google recently launched Boost, a location-based ad product. Boost is yet another product that Google is rolling out and so it may not be seen by everyone at this time. It was initially rolled out in San Francisco, Houston and Chicago. Boost ads show up when users search for local businesses in the sponsored links section of the search results.

To create a Boost Ad, simply go to the Google Places Dashboard. Initial setup is pretty easy, as you just set a budget like with regular PPC and the algorithm takes care of the details and the frequency.

Always be checking out the Google Places support area and blog for updates as to when these types of features are available in your area.

I have an assignment for you. Get on the Internet and try to find a negative review about your website. Respond to the review offering to make up for the customer's negative experience. If nothing comes of it, try again until you get an unhappy customer to respond. If you have no unhappy customers, great! You're golden. But, I want you to then respond to a happy customer, telling them how pleased you are that they had a great experience. Invite them in and offer them a discount or something free when they come in. I bet you they will write another positive review and tell 10 of their friends how awesome you are!

Bing Local

Creating a local listing with Bing involves a similar process to Google's. Start by going to the Bing Local Listing Center and click "Add new listing."

Then check if a listing for the business already exists and whether or not it has been claimed. If the business listing already exists, but is not claimed, go ahead and claim the listing. A verification postcard or phone call will provide a pin number just like with Google. The postcard can take a few weeks.

If the business listing doesn't already exist, Bing will require a Windows Live ID email address to be used or created.

Once logged in, complete the form with as much information as possible, ensuring that the information is the same as that on the business website and that, which was submitted for the Google Local Listing. The name of the business, address and phone number should always be submitted exactly the same way. This includes how the business suite number is referenced if that applies as well as how the business is spelled. For example, if you list "Vertical Measures, LLC" with Google and just "Vertical Measures" with Bing, you risk having the businesses be seen as separate when they're the same. Take every precaution to ensure that the search engines will view your business as the same across all of these listings.

Chapter 5
Citations and Link Building

Once you've optimized your website and set up your search engine local business listings, you're ready to start creating citations and links to your site. Most webmasters are familiar with SEO. It might not be their specialty, but they have likely heard of link building and know it's important to gain search engine rankings. But, what exactly is a citation and why are they crucial to your rankings?

Citations

Citations are to local search marketing as links are to search engine marketing. Citations are viewed by the local search engines as a listing of a business on a website, preferably with a matching address and phone number to that which is provided on the business website and on that search engine's local listing. Ideally, you have your complete address and local phone number on your website, you have claimed your search engine listings, and you have matching listings on sites like Yelp, CitySearch and Internet Yellow Page sites. The search engines see these listings as verification and as votes for your business. This will help your rankings in the local search results.

Now that the organic search results and local search results as well as the algorithms have been combined, link building must also be a part of a successful local search campaign. Many local search listing sites will allow you to include a link back to your website, a great way to build up your backlink profile while getting some good citations, essentially killing two birds with one stone. Local sites will have varying authority, strength and PageRanks. There are some great free tools to check out the stats on a website that provide you some insight as to how good of a link you're getting and how relevant the site is to your audience. Quantcast provides a lot of data including demographics and traffic for a website. Simply type in the URL of the site you're looking at and it gives results in just a few seconds.

Here, I've pulled up the data for Local.com.

To check the PageRank of a local listing site, SEOMoz has a toolbar, which also allows you to check if links are do-follow or no-follow. The toolbar is free and takes just seconds to download http://www.seomoz.org/seo-toolbar.

Creating citations can be time consuming and if you don't have the ability to hire an Internet marketing or local search marketing company, one of the fastest ways to get your business information out to the local search and directory sites is to submit your business to a service like **Universal Business Listing**. All you have to do is pay a fee and submit your business once. There are different levels of packages for Universal Business Listing. A business owner can choose to have UBL.org set up everything from the search engine listings to the various tiers of listings like the data aggregators and sites like Yelp and Merchant Circle. UBL.org does not claim listings until the Premium Package. Up until the Premium Package, UBL.org simply creates the listings and the business owner must still go and claim, verify and password protect those listings.

UBL.org has dozens of fields to fill in information for a business and also allows for submission of photos and videos. UBL.org also submits information to the major business data aggregators such as infoUSA, Express Update, Acxiom and D&B. The search engines crawl these sites to gather business data. So, if you see that your business is already listed on the search engines, these sites are very likely where the search engine got your information. But, always make sure that your listings are claimed and verified by you, the business owner!

Link Building

It's impossible to talk about anything related to Internet marketing without talking about link building. In addition to creating citations, a website must have a good variety of backlinks. This can be a full-time job in itself, as representatives at Google and other search engines continue to voice that links are still important and will continue to be in the future. Integrating link building for geospecific keywords can greatly improve local search marketing success. By now, you've done the keyword research and have created content on your site around those keywords. Now, build links to that content. There is a vast array of tactics that can build up your backlink profile including; article and/or press release marketing, manual link building, social media marketing, etc. Be sure to integrate link building tactics into your local search campaign or find a company that takes this holistic approach for best results.

Chapter 6
Customer Reviews and Check-In Sites

Location-based check-in and review services, such as Yelp, Foursquare and Gowalla are becoming increasingly popular with consumers around the world. Fortunately, these sites are also business-friendly, making it easy for business owners to engage with these sites' users. And, these sites should not be ignored as with the new Google Places results. Customer reviews are displayed more prominently than ever before and in many cases are affecting rankings in the Places results. Further, Google will displays reviews whether they are good or bad so it is important for a business owner to take advantage of this evolving space and engage with its customers.

This touches on online reputation management. ORM is a way through which you can control what shows up in the search results. If you have any negative reviews out on the Internet, providing positive reviews on your website can push down these negative reviews. Of course, I must encourage ethical practices here. Ask your happy customers if they can provide a review for you and if you can use their name. This will show authenticity and build trust amongst your customers and website visitors.

Reviews are the perfect platform for businesses to engage with their customers. Many businesses see reviews as a bad thing and wish they could just make them go away. But, why not use these to your advantage? If you receive a negative review and it's reasonable, you have a customer telling you exactly what you did wrong and therefore you have an opportunity to improve.

As the local search market continues to grow, so do the number of platforms and technologies with the purpose of allowing businesses to reward their loyal customers and drive more traffic to their brick and mortar locations. Incentives and rewards include; activity-based rewards, group check-in deals, frequency rewards as well as the ultra hip barcode scanning technology. Think about what is relevant and appropriate for your business before jumping into this space. Trying to have your hand in everything will not necessarily result in success, but picking the right platforms to engage on will provide you with great insight as to what your customers are saying about you and ultimately what they want from you.

These sites are continuously developing new features to out-do or stay relevant compared to the other. A great way to keep up with what is going on in this space is to subscribe to each site's blog. They all have one and frequently post news about new developments and features available to users and business owners. As you probably have already set up an email address for your local search marketing efforts, an easy way to keep your emails organized is to have these blog subscriptions sent to that email address as well. Do whatever works for you, but it is greatly beneficial to keep up with the latest news from these sites.

Yelp

While Yelp started primarily as a site for restaurant reviews, it has evolved to include businesses from a variety of industries. With well over a few million users and growing, Yelp has a free platform for business owners and therefore costs only your time to be listed there. With Yelp, business owners can engage with customers, read reviews about their business and offers deals and incentives for customers that check-in. The check-in offer feature was released in November 2010 to compete with Foursquare, Gowalla and Facebook Places.

Let's go through how to create a listing on Yelp:

1. First, just as you did with Google, you'll want to check if your business information is already on Yelp. Simply conduct a search for your business name and zip code to see if you're already there.

Here I've done a broad search for "Dog Store" in Phoenix, AZ. Most of the listings here have been claimed, but Pet Food Depot hasn't! If this were my business, I would select "Unlock.'

2. Create a Business Owners account for this business.

3. If your business is not listed, go to www.biz.yelp.com to create a business owner's account. This is different from a basic user account.

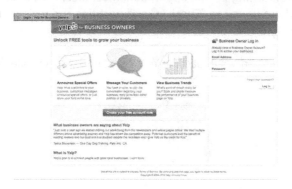

4. Create an optimized listing just as you did with Google.

5. Yelp will send you an email to verify your listing, and then you're set to go! Here is a business, Oh My Dog! in Phoenix that has a nice listing with some very positive reviews and four stars.

Do not fear negative reviews. They are going to happen and may be valid or invalid. Either way, take those as an opportunity to make those customers happy again. Write a response to the customers acknowledging their bad experience, offering to make it up to them in some way with perhaps a discount off their next visit.

In addition, even if your business receives a positive review, offer to have the guest return and treat them to a special as well. This will really drive home that your business appreciates its customers and strives to continue to provide superior service.

From the User Perspective

It is important to know how users will view your business and how they will interact with your listing on the application. Most local review sites have mobile applications where users can "Check In" and post tips and reviews. Each is slightly different, but very powerful.

Mobile users can download the Yelp App on to their mobile device.

Here is what the application looks like on my iPhone. Applications can vary slightly depending on what device you're using. As you can see, you can see what businesses are nearby, bookmark a review or business, check-in and much more.

Foursquare

Foursquare is another check-in application that continues to report record numbers for sign-ups and usage. In August 2010, Foursquare was closing in on 3 million users. Foursquare is an application that is primarily used via a mobile device. A user can check-in to a location and if that location is not listed with Foursquare, they can go ahead and list the business but cannot claim the business as the business owner. A postcard verification process must take place just like with Google

Places. Nevertheless, this application goes to show that your customers are out there talking about you, whether you are a part of the conversation or not.

With the Foursquare Mobile Application, customers can check-in to a restaurant and provide tips and reviews. When they check-in, they can also share this with their Facebook friends and Twitter followers, potentially sharing information about their experience with your business with thousands of people. Most people are competitive in nature. Foursquare provides various incentives for users to participate. There are different badges that a user can be rewarded with depending on the types of businesses they are checking in to. The list can be found here, and is actually very entertaining.

http://www.4squarebadges.com/foursquare-badge-list/

For example, there is the Bender Badge for those who check into bars four or more nights in a row. While it isn't necessarily something to brag about, people do find it humorous and tend to share that they've won a badge with their Facebook friends and Twitter followers. In addition to being rewarded badges, if a person checks into a location many times, more than any other individual on Foursquare, they can be declared Mayor. With being the Mayor comes great rewards, depending on the business owner. Often, businesses will provide the Mayor with offers and discounts each time they check-in. For example, a local Sports Authority in the Phoenix area provides $10 off any item to the Mayor when he or she checks in. Just like with any coupon or discount, this should ultimately lead to that individual coming back to the store repeatedly and telling their friends about it.

Let's go through how to create a listing on Foursquare:

1.   Go to www.foursquare.com/businesses

2.   Search for your business to see if it has already been listed. Foursquare users are able to submit a business to Foursquare, but only the business owner can claim the listing and control things such as coupons and specials.

3. If a business has not been claimed, a verification process must occur. Foursquare only does postcard verification. The postcard should arrive within a couple of weeks and will have a verification code that must be entered to start creating specials, discounts, etc.

4. Once you've claimed the Foursquare listing, start taking advantage of all Foursquare has to offer.

You can review stats for activity at your business, such as who is checking in, how many times and when.

A business owner can also create Foursquare specials based on a variety of metrics. There are many possibilities.

Mayor Specials: unlocked only by the Mayor of the business. The Mayor is considered the single most loyal customer, checking in the most times over the past 60 days.

Your Mayor special might read:

You're the Mayor of Dan's Bakery! Enjoy a free chocolate chip cookie each time you check-in!

Check-in Specials: unlocked when a user checks in to your venue a certain number of times.

Your check-in special might read:

You've checked in here 10 times! Enjoy a free drink today.

Frequency-based Specials: are unlocked every X check-ins.

Your frequency-based special might read:

Foursquare users get 20% off any entree every 5th check-in!

Wildcard Specials: always unlocked, but your staff has to verify some extra conditions before awarding the Special.

Show us your foursquare Swarm badge and get a free drink!

Foursquare is often rolling out updates and new features for users and business owners.

Google HotPot

To further drive home the importance of reviews, Google created its own review site, HotPot.

Google HotPot is Google's recommendation engine for local and has proven to influence search results in Places and Maps. A user can create a profile and rate and review businesses and services. The user can choose to display their name and picture or not. HotPot users build up their friends list, usually selected from your Gmail friend list. The goal here is for Google to surface reviews from your HotPot friends, creating a more personal user experience.

Facebook Places

Facebook entered the location check-in scene in September 2010. Facebook Places is similar to the others, allowing Facebook users to check in to any place in Facebook's Places database, powered by Localeze. Check-ins are shared on a user's Facebook wall and in their friends' feeds.

Business owners can claim their Facebook Places page with a similar verification process as Google Places. Facebook Places is integrated into the mobile application of Facebook as well.

While Facebook Places does not yet compete directly with the business owner platform of Yelp and Foursquare, the numbers put Facebook in good position to do so. Facebook has over 150 million mobile users and 1.5 million existing local business fan pages, which are being phased into Place pages.

The process of creating a Facebook Places page can be a little tricky.

1.   If no one has checked into your company's venue, you will need to have an iPhone or Smartphone and load the Facebook Places applica-

tion to check if your Places page already exists. Do this by searching for your business in the search box. If it does not exist, click Add.

2. Facebook will then automatically list your local phone number. You can change it if it is incorrect.

3. Then, log into Facebook and search for the Place that you just created. Once you find the venue, at the bottom of the Place page, it will say "If this is your business, claim it now."

You will need to receive a phone call from Facebook as well. It allows you to put a direct extension if needed.

And lastly, it is generally not recommended to merge your Place page and your Business page. Many have complained of loss of functionality of their Business page. The Places page at this time, should be set up and claimed so that customers may check-in and share this with their friends, not necessarily as a marketing tool like your Business page.

The Future of Check-In Applications

While Facebook Places has room to grow as far as the functionality of the application and benefits for business owners, Facebook's entrance to the space pushes this check-in application to a half a billion users and many advertisers. Many users who cringed at the idea of having one more social network are getting comfortable with the idea via Facebook and will likely move to Foursquare and Yelp as well, if they haven't already.

With most of these social check-in and review applications, a user can engage with a business whether the business owner has claimed or verified the list or not. Therefore, it is important to control the information listed about your business. While you cannot control which reviews and ratings appear, you can ensure that all of the details about your business are accurate and see what your customers are saying about you. This information is priceless. A business owner can track sales, demographic and psychographic information, but it is invaluable to know how customers feel about your business and what they are telling their friends about you.

Chapter 7
Tracking Local Search Success with Google Analytics

Knowing where your traffic is coming from can provide great insights as to what is working and what is not. After all of that hard work to implement a local search campaign it feels great to see the traffic coming in from the various channels you've created.

Here are just a few of the ways that you can track traffic coming from the search engines as well as local listing sites. Your local traffic can be tracked by creating advanced segments and by adding a new search engine, maps.google.com.

You can track:

- Traffic from Search Engines by Geospecific Keyword Phrase
- Traffic from Google Maps Subdomain
- Traffic from Regions
- Traffic from Local Listing Sites

Google Analytics has more features and capabilities than many are aware of, providing massive amounts of valuable information and it is worth going through the course that Google offers through Conversion University at www.conversion-university.com.

Advanced segments can be applied to historical data and are available across all of your Google Analytics accounts and profiles.

We'll cover the first case, how to track traffic from geospecific searches from the search engines.

Traffic from Search Engines by Geospecific Keyword Phrases

By creating this advanced segment in Google Analytics, you will be able to track what geospecific keyword phrases users are searching for when they go to your website.

1. Login to your Google Analytics Dashboard.

2. Click on Advanced Segments in the left navigation of Google Analytics, then click on the 'Default Segments' area to open up the list of the built-in Segments. You can use these as the starting point for building a custom segment.

3. Click the 'Copy' link to the right of "Non-paid Search Traffic." This will open up the configuration screen for the segment so that you can make changes and then save it as a new segment.

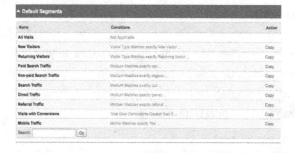

4. Name the Segment something related to the traffic you're tracking. A good name for tracking traffic from search engines with keyword phrases like "phoenix shoe store" might be "Phoenix Search Traffic."

5. Then, click the "Add 'or' Statement"" button, because what you want is a segment where all the visits are from organic search "and" the keywords used for the search were part of your target group.

6. Next, open up the green "Dimensions" menu on the left hand side of the screen and drag the "Keyword" dimension over in to the report area and drop it on the "dimension or metric" box.

7. Add Keyword List: At this point there are two ways to add your keyword list. With the drag and drop option, type in your first keyword in the box to the right of the keyword dimension. For precise matching, use the "Matches Exactly" default option or you may choose "Contains". With "Matches Exactly", you'll want to type in your exact keyword phrase. To capture all variations with the keyword Phoenix, use 'Contains.

8. Then, add your keyword variations. To do this you need to 'Add an "or" statement'. Be careful about this. You need to add the 'Or' to the list of keywords, not to the 'Medium'. Be sure to use the 'Add an "or" statement' link beneath the keywords.

You may also use a regular expression. To do this, you only need to add one instance of the keyword match statement, then click the drop down menu to the right of the 'keyword' dimension and change it from the default 'Matches Exactly' to 'Matches Regular Expression.'

A simple way to add multiple keywords is to separate each of the keywords with a pipe character. It can be found above the \ character just north of the Enter key (Return on a Mac). The pipe character simply means *or*.

For example it would look like this: Phoenix | Scottsdale | Mesa, etc.

The grey border area around these input areas shows how they are grouped together. You can then repeat this adding of and 'or' statement for each of the keywords in your list.

9. In addition, you'll want to narrow down where the traffic is coming from. Click Add "and" statement and drop "Source" into the metric box. Then select all of the search engines for which you wish to track, most importantly the ones you've created a local listing with.

Be sure to Test Segment before creating to ensure you've properly set it up.

Then, go back to your dashboard and you'll be able to view the report for this segment and see what traffic you're getting from the search engines for geospecific keyword phrase

Conclusion

Local search marketing has become very complex, even more so with the local results being mixed in with the organic. Local can no longer be considered a separate effort from your online marketing campaign. Link building, press release marketing, content development and other online marketing tactics can all be incorporated into a local search marketing campaign. It must be a holistic approach in order to succeed.

This book has provided you with a jumping off point, a systematic plan to get started. Now get out there are start claiming what you already own, your business and start driving more targeted traffic to your website and to your storefront today!

BONUS: Need to Know Local Search Terms

As the local search industry continues to grow, so does the terminology! While there are certain terms and phrases that are standard across the industry, there are some that are less commonly used or have alternative terms. Below is a list that might help you navigate your way through the streets of local search and in the process provide a basic understanding of local search marketing.

Category: When listing your business with Google Places especially, you will want to choose a category for your business. This is a very important factor in their algorithm. If you have not claimed your business on Google Places, it will choose a category for you from a set of approximately 2,000 default business types based on the North American Industry Classification System. Be sure to select the correct category for your business and up to 4 subcategories to be sure the search engines know what your business is all about.

Centroid: As determined by the local search engines, the centroid is the very center of a neighborhood or metropolitan area.

Citation: Citations are to local search optimization as links are to website search engine optimization. Citations are an online mention of a business, ideally with location-based information such as the business name, address and phone number that matches the information on the business' own website.

Data Provider, Aggregator, IYP: Companies such as infoUSA, Localeze, and Superpages are major data providers, also known as data aggregators and Internet Yellow Pages. The search engines often crawl these sites to gather business data. So, if you see that your business is already listed on the search engines, these sites are very likely where the search engine got your information. You will want to claim your listings to ensure all the information is correct.

Directory: A website that lists business contact information in an organized manner, typically in alphabetical order and/or by business type. Just as the search engines look to data providers and aggregators to gather information, they also crawl directories.

Geospecific search: When a user searches for a business or company with a geographic modifier such as a city, state or zip code. For example, "plumbers, San Diego, CA".

Review: A customer's summary of his/or experience with a particular business. Reviews cannot be controlled by the business owner. Reviews can be left on Google Places and on most other local search listing sites like Yelp, Foursquare and

Gowalla. Business owners should pay attention to these reviews and use reviews as an opportunity to engage with customers. This touches on online reputation management.

This list covers the basic terminology that you will likely hear when you start talking to a local search professional. Knowing these terms will get you on your way to having a better understanding of local search.

BIBLIOGRAPHY

Mihm, David. "Local Search Ranking Factors 2010: Volume 3" 7 June 2010
< http://www.davidmihm.com/local-search-ranking-factors.shtml>

www.ingramcontent.com/pod-product-compliance
Lightning Source LLC
Chambersburg PA
CBHW061042050326
40689CB00012B/2941